WHEN THEY
BROKE DOWN THE DOOR

Poems

Fatemeh Shams

Introduced and Translated by
Dick Davis

MAGE PUBLISHERS

Copyright © 2016 Mage Publishers

All rights reserved.
No part of this book may be reproduced
or retransmitted in any manner whatsoever,
except in the form of a review, without the
written permission of the publisher.

LIBRARY OF CONGRESS CATALOGING-IN-PUBLICATION DATA
DETAILS AVAILABLE AT THE LIBRARY OF CONGRESS

First paperback original edition
ISBN: 978-1-933823-80-5

First eBook edition

202-342-1642 • as@mage.com
Visit Mage online www.mage.com

To Mazlinda and Rowena,
without them I would not have survived in exile.

فهرست

مشهد	.	.	.	۲
در را که شکستند	.	.	۴
هرگز نخوابیدن	.	.	۶
سه سال بعد	.	.	۸
به تدریج	.	.	۱۰
شرط بند	.	.	۱۲
پناهنده	.	.	۱۴
دو لیوان مرگ	.	.	۱۶
خاکستر و مه	.	.	۱۸
اعتراف	.	.	۲۰
مجسمه	.	.	۲۲
جیم مثل جنگ (۱)	.	۲۴
جیم مثل جنگ (۲)	.	۲۶
کاش	.	.	۲۸
ماهی‌گیر	.	.	۳۰
در جستجوی وطن	.	۳۲
باتلاق	.	.	۳۴
چیزهایی برای گفتن	.	۳۶
خانه	.	.	۴۰
جزیره	.	.	۴۲
فصل جنون	.	.	۴۴
آفرینش	.	.	۴۶
یواشکی	.	.	۴۸
مسافر	.	.	۵۰

حتی اگر هرگز نباشی	.	۵۲
پالتو	.	.	۵۴
گوهردشت	.	.	۵۶
محبوس	.	.	۵۸
پیاده	.	.	۶۰
جنین	.	.	۶۲
اندوه خاموش	.	.	۶۴
به رنگ آتش	.	.	۶۶
حقیقت	.	.	۶۸
بیگانه	.	.	۷۰
صدف‌ها	.	.	۷۲
بهاریه ۹۴	.	.	۷۴
غزل رفتن	.	.	۷۶
از آن روزها	.	.	۷۸
تا که در آغوشت	.	.	۸۰
تعقیب	.	.	۸۲
دورنیست	.	.	۸۴
غزه	.	.	۸۶
فشنگ سرگردان	.	۹۰
اسیدپاشی	.	.	۹۲
جیم مثل جنگ (۳)	.	۹۴
شعری برای ایران	.	۹۸
ریشه‌ها	.	.	۱۰۲

Contents

MASHHAD 3

WHEN THEY BROKE DOWN
THE DOOR 5

NEVER TO FALL ASLEEP . . 7

THREE YEARS LATER . . . 9

GRADUALLY 11

THE WAGER 13

THE REFUGEE 15

TWO GLASSES OF DEATH . 17

ASH AND MIST 19

CONFESSION 21

STATUE 23

W FOR WAR (1) 25

W FOR WAR (2) 27

I WISH 29

FISHERMAN 31

IN SEARCH OF A HOMELAND 33

THE MARSH 35

THINGS TO SAY . . . 37

HOME 41

ISLAND 43

THE SEASON OF MADNESS . 45

CREATION 47

STEALTHILY 49

TRAVELLER 51

EVEN IF YOU'RE NEVER
TO BE HERE 53

OVERCOAT 55

GOWHAR DASHT . . . 57

BLOCKED OFF 59

ON FOOT 61

THE FETUS 63

SILENT SORROW . . . 65

THE COLOR OF FIRE . . 67

TRUTH 69

STRANGER 71

SHELLS 73

SPRING '94 75

LEAVING 77

FROM THOSE DAYS . . 79

UNTIL I'M IN YOUR ARMS . 81

PROSECUTION 83

AMPHIBIOUS 85

GAZA 87

WANDERING BULLET . . 91

ACID-THROWING . . . 93

W FOR WAR (3) 95

A POEM FOR IRAN . . . 99

ROOTS 103

Introduction

Countries with a history of absolutist or despotic government tend also to have a tradition of politicized poetry; this is especially noticeable in the poetry of the last two centuries, when an alternative to despotism became at least imaginable and perhaps feasible. In some countries however the tradition can reach much further back, and this is particularly true of the literary history of Iran which provides numerous examples of the association of poetry and often impotent political anger; the link arguably dates back as far as the eleventh-century epic *The Shahnameh* with its recurrent cry for justice against cruel or incompetent kings, and is clearly evident in poetry written in prison, a practice that has continued from the early medieval period (the first major example is that of the poet Mas'ud Sa'd, who lived from 1046 to 1121) to this day. In the work of Iranian women poets this linking of politics and poetry has often been joined by a third area of concern, that of erotic passion, an association that runs through the work of women poets from other linguistic and national traditions, as for example in the despairing heroism of the great Russian poets Marina Tsetayeva and

Anna Akhmatova. It is an association that may at first sight seem counter-intuitive – the privacy of erotic passion allied with the public stance of political protest – but the link is of course that both the passion and the politics are subversive of the status quo – of patriarchy that would deny women erotic autonomy, and of political authority that would deny them social freedom.

In the Iranian case, although the roots of this trio of poetry, politics, and passion in women's writing reach deep into literary history (they go at least as far back as the fourteenth-century poet Jahan Khatun for example, and more recently to the nineteenth-century Babi poet, Qorrat al-Ayn, also known as Tahereh), the iconic exponent of this juxtaposition has been Forugh Farrokhzad (1935-1967), the most widely read and admired Iranian woman poet of the twentieth century. The blatant eroticism of Farrokhzad's poems shocked her own generation of readers, and although the subversive political implications of her verse were usually fairly muted they were nevertheless clear to the majority of her audience. Patriarchy and political authority were under scrutiny in her work, which also incorporated another kind of heady rebellion, this time against the traditional structures of verse itself, as her poetry was written in the at the time relatively new form of *"she'r-e no"* (free verse). Her example has proved almost irresistible to the women poets who have succeeded her, and this has been particularly true of those who have come to prominence since the Iranian Revolution of 1979, many of whom have had to exile themselves from their homeland, and who evoke the emotional turmoil of exile with heartfelt eloquence. So compelling has Forugh

Farrokhzad's example been to these post-revolutionary woman poets that the critic Ahmad Karimi Hakkak, the most insightful and comprehensive guide to the Iranian poetry of the last hundred years, has dubbed them, "The Daughters of Forugh" ("*Dokhtaran-e Forugh*").

But it goes without saying that while literary traditions and political upheavals can provide the context for individual poets, it is their individuality itself – the specific nature of this poet's work, in these words, coming out of these particular circumstances – that is the lodestone that draws us to any given poet, and keeps us coming back to her. In attempting to provide a quick sketch of their literary and political contexts, I do not wish in any way to imply that the poems by the poet in this book are exhaustively defined by such contexts; Fatemeh Shams is her own poet with her own themes, style, and language, broadly categorizable perhaps within the general flow of contemporary Iranian literary history, but distinctively and memorably hers, and hers alone.

Shams was born in 1983 into a professional middle class family (her father is a judge, her mother a lawyer) in Mashhad, the chief city of the province of Khorasan in northeastern Iran, and the second most important city in the country for Shia pilgrimage, as it contains the tomb of Imam Reza, the eighth Shia Imam. She has written that the most important influence on her young life was that of her maternal grandmother, by whom she was largely brought up, and who died when Fatemeh was sixteen; for Shams, "her loss remains the biggest loss in my whole life." Like teenagers everywhere – and this seems particularly true of those in Iran – she caught the poetry bug early, but its effects lingered instead of quickly wearing off as it does with most adolescents. She read avidly and widely, even though accessing poetry collections was not easy for a fifteen-year-old student in a conservative city, but first through her mother's neglected library in the cellar of their house, and then with the aid of her literature teacher at the high school, she became familiar with the work of what were to be her favorite twentieth century poets – Ahmad Shamlou, Mehdi Akhavan-Sales, Esmail Khoi, and – naturally – Forugh Farrokhzad. And, equally naturally, she began to write her own poems. She wrote with such fluency that when she showed her mother some of her early efforts, her mother asked her if she hadn't copied them from someone else, in effect stolen them. By the age of sixteen, Shams had won the silver medal in a National Olympiad of Literature, for which she traveled to Tehran, the capital. This proved to be a life-changing journey for her, as "During those eighteen days, I met leading poets, writers and critics for the first time, and made up my mind that I would dedicate the rest of my life to poetry and literature." Against her parents' will, she moved to Tehran more permanently a year later to begin university studies in literature, although like poets in many parts of the world she found the way it was taught in the university to be stultifying, and she soon changed her major to sociology even though literature remained her chief private passion.

Despite the fact that the poets she read so avidly as a teenager all wrote in free verse, Shams's early poems were often cast in the traditional form of the *ghazal*, and she has continued to write poems in both traditional forms and free verse throughout her life. Although there is not an absolute correlation between particular forms and particular kinds of content in her work she tends to use free form (as Ahmad Karimi-Hakkak has pointed out) largely for self communing, meditative poems and traditional forms for more outspoken statements of conviction and/or defiance (erotic or political). A writer whom she came to appreciate a little later than her adolescent enthusiasms was the major woman poet Simin Behbahani, and it may well be Behbahani's example that encouraged her to continue to write on contemporary subjects in traditional forms; when Behbahani died in 2015 Shams wrote at least two poems and two obituaries in her memory, clearly indicating the importance of the older poet's example to her own work. Behbahani's passionate patriotism maintained against all odds, and her urge to fight for the freedom of Iranian women, made her a great source of inspiration for Shams who was deeply engaged with the political scene at University of Tehran during her studies for her undergraduate degree. These political involvements led to the issuing of a warrant for her arrest following disturbances at Tehran University in 2004 when she fled the capital and spent three months in her hometown, Mashhad. The turmoil, however, did not put an end to her engagement with the student movement, which has continued up to the present.

After graduating from Tehran University she moved to England to pursue a degree in History and Muslim Civilization at the Aga Khan University in London. Up to this point the political and social realities of life in Iran, while clearly part of the context in which she had grown up and informing the content of many of her early poems, had not seemed especially shocking or thought-provoking to her — they were simply the reality surrounding her childhood and youth. All this was to change after the Iranian presidential election of 2009 when the Iranian Green Movement arose in response to what was widely seen as the fraudulent re-election as President of Mahmoud Ahmadinejad. Major demonstrations occurred in the chief cities of Iran, forming the largest street protests (it was claimed by Al-Jazeera) since the Iranian Revolution of 1979 that had brought Ayatollah Khomeini to power. The unrest was repressed with considerable violence and numerous protestors were killed by security forces; the Green Movement's leaders as well as many of its rank-and-file followers were arrested and many sentenced to long periods of solitary confinement. Among those arrested and imprisoned were a number of people close to Shams, including her younger sister; Shams's own writings in support of the movement, and of human-rights activists within and outside of the country, meant that she could no longer return to Iran, and she became a de facto exile. Her eight-year relationship with her partner foundered under the strain, and this, together with her sister's imprisonment, can be considered her most personal casualties of the uprising. When her first book of poems was published in 2013 it was called 1388 (equivalent to 2009 in the Western calendar), the Persian year of the contested election and the Green Movement's subsequent appearance and repression; as the book's title clearly indicated, politics had moved to the center stage of her poetry.

But in reading her poems it is important to realize that this political preoccupation does not arise from any ideological stance, and it would be irrelevant to compare her to an ideologically committed political poet such as, for example, Bertolt Brecht. It is the personal, the intimately human, that informs her poetry, not the ideological. In an interview published in 2012, Shams described her approach as "outside of the structure of active party participation," she stated that she is "a supporter of no political party," and that the political concerns of her poetry come from the fact that ". . . in a country like Iran where politics has penetrated into the smallest and most intimate details of life it is unavoidable." Her poetry comes most strikingly out of a response to human suffering, that of others and her own, and one of the reasons that politics is so omnipresent in many of her poems is that it is seen as the chief cause of such suffering. It is not humanity en masse about and for whom she writes, and certainly she does not even hint at communal ideological solutions to human distress; her focus is the misery and travail of an individual caught up in political processes and structures that are contemptuous of individuals. It is this focus on the individual that accounts for the importance of love poetry in her oeuvre (and in this she is similar to the two Russian "political" poets mentioned above, Tsetayeva and Akhmatova); in their fundamental inwardness and privacy the passions of love constitute the value most obviously opposed to the demands of group-think and the social constraints that political ideology demands. It is no coincidence that one of Shams's best-known poems, which is the title poem of this book, describes exactly that moment when the brutality of mass politics destroys the privacy of personal passion. In the same interview quoted above, she said that during the dark days of her exile it has been poetry that has saved her, and clearly for her, poetry – despite the political implications of her own verse – is something inward and personal rather than public and propagandistic, and when asked whether she saw herself more as a political activist or as a poet she replied that poetry for her is "the more meaningful activity." The title of her doctorate, which she completed at Oxford in 2015, is "The Social History of Poetry after the Iranian Revolution," and it is largely the misuse of poetry for purposes of political propaganda on which she focuses.

A NOTE ON THE TRANSLATIONS

In translating Fatemeh Shams's poems from *1388* and from her second book *Writing in the Mist* (*Neveshtan dar Meh*, published in 2015), I have corresponded extensively with Ms. Shams. Our usual method has been for me to send her a first draft, for Ms. Shams to comment on this and to make suggestions and objections, and for me to modify my draft accordingly. The first draft of very few poems survived as the final draft, and sometimes the back and forth went on through numerous revisions and rewritings, to the extent that a more honest description of the process in many cases would be "Translated by Fatemeh Shams and Dick Davis," rather than simply "Translated by Dick Davis." For the poems in traditional forms I have tried to imitate at least some aspects of the form in the English versions, in so far as this is possible; in a number of cases this has been managed with some accuracy, but sometimes the English versions contain not much more than a structural gesture to indicate something of the formal nature of the original.

Poems

مشهد

من از شهرِ کافه‌های گردن زده می‌آیم
از شهرِ خانه‌های مشبّک
از شهرِ میدانِ اعدام قدیم و میدانِ شهدای جدید
از تلاقی‌گاه دود سیگار و بال فرشتگان
بر سربازخانه نام قرارگاه گذاشته بودند
و نه اسمی بر بی‌قراری سربازهای دیده بانِ آلوده به دو تار موی
زن
دو تار!
من از شهرِ آوازه‌خوان‌های گردن کش‌می‌آیم
از محل شهادتِ خودم
مشهد.

MASHHAD

I come from a town of beheaded closed cafés
from a town of latticed houses
from a town whose old execution square is now called
   Martyrs' Square
from the meeting place of cigarette smoke and angels' wings
they've named the barracks The Resting Place
which makes no reference to the Restlessness of the Sentries
polluted by two strands of a woman's hair
two strands!
I come from the town of stubborn singers
from the place of my own martyrdom
Mashhad.

در را که شکستند

در را که شکستند در آغوش تو بودم
لالایی سرمازده در گوش تو بودم
در را که شکستند مرا سخت فشردی
در آن شب وحشت‌زده، تن‌پوش تو بودم
زیر لگد و فحش، تو عریان و من عریان
خونابه‌چکان تن بیهوش تو بودم
افتادی و آرام نگاه تو فرو ریخت
انگار که صد سال، فراموش تو بودم
وقتی که تو را بردند، یک نغمه‌ی غمگین
دریای پری‌هایِ خاموشِ تو بودم
یک بغض ترک‌خورده‌ی آرام، میانِ
پرونده‌ی تاخورده و مخدوش تو بودم
هر چند تو را دار کشیدند عزیزم
در حافظه‌ی عکس، هم‌آغوش تو بودم.

WHEN THEY BROKE DOWN THE DOOR

When they broke down the door I was in your arms
Like a freezing cold lullaby curled in your ear

When they broke down the door you gripped me tightly,
I was the clothes on your body, on that night filled with fear

Beneath their kicks and their curses you were naked and I
    was naked
I was your body, dripping blood, unconscious, my dear

You fell, and your calm gaze faltered and failed,
As though I were something you'd forgotten, year after year

When they took you I was a grief-stricken cry,
A silent sea where your fabulous creatures appear

I was a sadness cracked open, calm in the midst
Of your file that was folded now, smudged and unclear

And though they have hanged you, in memory's
Image, I see myself there, in your arms, my dear.

꒰ꞈ

هرگز نخوابیدن

از ترس یک کابوس تا هرگز نخوابیدن
هر شب نشستن تا طلوع صبح را دیدن
جایی میان خواب و بیداری، تلو خوردن
در برزخ کوری به نام زندگی مُردن

در جا زدن در عشق‌های پوچ تکراری
در دوستت دارم عزیزم! دوستم داری؟
در خواستن‌هایی که از دم بی‌سرانجامند
در شغل‌های آبکی، در قعر بیکاری

بی‌حافظه، بی‌مرز، بی شهر و وطن بودن
آواره در آغوش سرد مرد و زن بودن
یک ساک و سیصد جلد را هی جا به جا کردن
بین تمام رنگ‌ها، رنگ کفن بودن

دل کندن از هر کس که بر صورت نقابی داشت
هر کس که در قعر وجودش منجلابی داشت
دل کندن از شهر غریب کودکی‌هایم
آنجا که در خاک‌اش غم و اندوه نابی داشت

از برنگشتن‌های بی‌پایان پُر تردید
بیدارخوابی بی تو در آغوش این تبعید
دلتنگی بی‌مرز از هرگز ندیدن‌ها
سرخوردگی از ابتذال واژه امید

بی‌سرزمین، بی‌عشق، در اوج همین مستی
در کوچه‌ی باریک بی پایان بن‌بستی
آوردنت بالا و هی با عشق پرسیدن
ای سرزمین خسته! توی فکر من هستی؟

NEVER TO FALL ASLEEP

Never to fall sleep, because of a nightmare's fear
To sit awake each night until the dawn is here
Caught between waking and sleep, as if unsteady with drink,
In the name of life to die, with blindness drawing near

In futile empty love repeated endlessly
In saying, "I love you, my dear! Do you love me?"
In wanting things that reach their end but never start,
In pointless work, in no work's sour banality

To have no memory, no border, and no place,
To be unhoused in men's and women's cold embrace,
To drag with you a suitcase and three hundred books
To have, among all colors, a shroud's conceal your face

To tear my heart from those who wore a mask and
    all they mean,
From men whose inward being is a reeking foul latrine,
To tear my heart from that strange city of my childhoods '
Whose earth holds sorrow still that's innocent and clean

From endless hesitating, from not returning there,
In waking dreams without you, in exile's arms and air,
In boundless longing for the things I'll never see,
In "hope," that lovely word whose absence brings despair

Without a homeland, without love, in wild perplexity,
Within this narrow cul-de-sac from which I can't walk free
To vomit you from me, and ah to ask you with my love
"Oh wounded, worn-out country! Do you still think of me?"

سه سال بعد

اینجا . . . هجوم وحشی باران، سه سال بعد
تلخ و غریب و خسته و ویران، سه سال بعد
شب‌های بی‌قراری تهران، سه سال قبل
کابوس‌های تلخ خیابان، سه سال بعد
معکوس می‌شمارم و نابود می‌شود
حسی درون این تن بی‌جان، سه سال بعد
از لحظه‌های سخت پریدن . . . فرودگاه
تا نامه‌های پاره‌ی زندان، سه سال بعد
از عشق بی‌بهانه و احساس سوخته
تا ترس و درد و گریه و هذیان، سه سال بعد
از شک و کفر و دین و یقین، سبز یا که سرخ
تا مست و تلخ و سرد و گریزان، سه سال بعد
از گم شدن کنار خیابان، سه سال قبل
تا گورهای مخفی و ویران سه سال بعد
از کوچ ناگهانی و مرگ هَزارها
تا بازگشت شوم کلاغان، سه سال بعد

سهم من از نبودن او، قاب عکس شد
اینجا کنار طاقچه، مامان، سه سال بعد
آتش گرفته خاطره‌هایم ولی هنوز
خاکسترم سراسر و سوزان، سه سال بعد
شاید دوباره شعر شود لحظه‌های من.
در کوچه‌باغ‌های خراسان، سه سال بعد.

THREE YEARS LATER

Here . . . the violent pelting of rain, three years later
Bitter and broken, foreign, in pain, three years later

The unsettling nights in Tehran, three years before
The road's bitter nightmares made plain, three years later

I count them backwards, they disappear
In this soulless body their traces remain, three years later

From the difficult moments of flight . . . the airport
To torn letters from prison I still retain, three years later

From love without excuses and a sense of burning and ruin
To fear and tears, delirium and pain, three years later

From doubt and blasphemy, faith and certainty, green or red
To flight and bewilderment, cold, bitter, inane, three years
    later

From someone missing at the roadside, three years before
To the destroyed, hidden graves of the slain, three years later

From sudden flight and thousands of deaths
To the hideous crows returning again, three years later

What is left for me now from my mother is her photograph,
There on the shelf, in its frame, three years later

My memories have gone up in flames, but everywhere
The burning ashes still remain, three years later
Perhaps my moments will become a poem
On garden paths in Khorasan again, three years later.

به تدریج

در کوچه صدای قدم باد، به تدریج
گم می‌شود از حافظه‌ام یاد، به تدریج
در کوچه کسی نیست و این جسم تهی را
با خویش سفر می‌برد این باد، به تدریج
هی می‌گذرم، فصل به فصل از سر این درد
از خاطره‌ی مبهم خرداد، به تدریج
بر لاشه‌ی تقویم کپک‌بسته به دیوار
یخ بسته تن زخمی اعداد، به تدریج
در سیطره‌ی ساکت و پرهول زمانیم
در قحطی نان، گم شده فریاد، به تدریج
هر کس نفسی داشت به چنگ قفس افتاد
ویرانه شد آن خانه‌ی آباد، به تدریج
می‌خواستم آرام از این درد بمیرم
از این همه ویرانی و بیداد، به تدریج
ما ساکت و خاموش از این قصّه گذشتیم
شمشیر سپردیم به جلاد، به تدریج.

GRADUALLY

In the alley, the sound of the wind's steps gradually
Fades from my memory, my mind, gradually

There is no one in the alley, and the wind
Has taken this empty body on its journey, gradually

Season by season, I get past the pain
Of that June's confused memories, gradually

In the leaves of a musty calendar stuck to the wall
Those wounded, numbered days, a body frozen in ice,
    gradually

In the reign of silence, the shocks handed me by time,
In the absence of bread, cries became lost, gradually

Anyone who breathed fell into that cage's clutches
And the house crumbled into ruin, gradually

I wanted to die in peace from this pain
From all these ruins and injustice, gradually

Quietly, in silence, we left this story behind
And handed the executioner his sword, gradually.

شرط بند

ما زنده بودیم، اما، در لاک خود مرده بودیم
ما حرف‌های مگو را با بغض‌مان خورده بودیم
ما زنده بودیم، اما، تنها و دلتنگ و خاموش
از داغ‌هایی که دیدیم، ویران و سرخورده بودیم
ما شانه بودیم و آغوش، ما اشک بودیم و فریاد
تنها در این شهر غربت، بر زخم خود گُرده بودیم
حتی اگر ترس و وحشت در جان‌مان لانه می‌کرد
اما به ویرانی خویش ایمان نیاورده بودیم
ما ایستادیم و مردیم تا زندگی جان بگیرد
در گور تنهایی خویش ما شرط را برده بودیم.

THE WAGER

We were alive, but within ourselves we had died
We'd choked down the outlawed words we were forced
  to hide

We were alive, but silent, alone, and homesick,
Disheartened by the scars we'd endured side by side

We were shoulders, embraces, tears, and our cries, alone
In a strange town, suffering the wounds that we bore inside

And though horror and fear made their nest in our souls
We would not believe in our loss, defeat was denied

We stood and we died so that life would take hold, making
The wager, in this solitary grave where we've died.

پناهنده

سقوطِ ارزشِ آدم، سقوطِ آینده
سقوطِ کشتیِ یک کودکِ پناهنده
سقوطِ دستِ عروسک به عمقِ اقیانوس
به عمقِ فاصله‌هایِ به مرگ آکنده
سقوطِ پایِ پیاده به سمتِ کوهستان
سقوطِ عاطفه در مرزهایِ بازنده
دو بالِ سوخته سهمِ کمیست از دنیا
پرنده‌هایِ مهاجر، بدون پرونده
پرنده‌هایِ مهاجر، به سمت هیچ‌کجا
پرنده‌هایِ گُمِ هر کجا پراکنده
که کوله‌پشتیِ سنگین‌شان پر از درد است
که کوله‌پشتی‌شان بی‌بهار و بی‌خنده
وطن، گذشته‌یِ غمگینِ بی‌سرانجامیست
وطن: سقوطِ غم‌انگیز یک پناهنده.

THE REFUGEE

The loss of a person's worth, his future lost in those seas,
The loss of the boat of a child of refugees

The loss of a doll's hand in the depths of the ocean,
In the depths of its death-filled profundities

The loss of a step on the way to the mountains
The luckless at the borders, the loss of all kindnesses

Two burned wings are little enough from the world
   to have,
Migratory birds, with no visas overseas

Migratory birds on the way to nowhere, birds
Scattered and lost in nowhere's immensities

Their backpacks are empty of spring and of laughter
Their backpacks are heavy with pain, uneasy anxieties

Homeland is a sad past with no end
Homeland: the heart-breaking loss of the refugees.

دو لیوان مرگ

این روزها دلتنگ و خاموشم کمابیش
با نعش خود هر شب هماغوشم کمابیش
گز می‌کنم میخانه‌ها را، کافه‌ها را
روزی دو لیوان مرگ می‌نوشم کمابیش
دور از تو باری بر دلم، بر پلک‌هایم
هفتاد مَن بُغض است بر دوشم کمابیش
دیوارهای خانه سیم خاردارند
شلیک تیری دور، در گوشم کمابیش
این روزها، دلتنگ؟ نه! خاموش هم نه
یک شعرِ بی‌پایان مغشوشم کمابیش.

TWO GLASSES OF DEATH

I'm homesick and silent, these days, more or less
I sleep in my own corpse's arms, each night, more or less

I wander to bars and cafés; each day
I drink down two glasses of death, more or less

Far from you, the weight on my heart, my eyelids,
  my shoulders
Is like seventy measures of grief, more or less

The walls of the house are barbed wire
From far off there's gunfire, in my ears more or less

These days homesick? No! And not silent
But a poem that's endless, unraveling more or less.

خاکستر و مه

چطور بگویم؟
اینها را نمی‌شود شعر کرد
چیزی مثل آن شب که
دست در حجم خاکستری موهاش بردم
و کل خیابان
حتی اتوبوسی که از دور می‌آمد
آتش گرفت.

ASH AND MIST

How can I say this?
these aren't things a poem can be made from
something like that night when
my hand touched the mass of your ashen hair
and the whole street
even the bus approaching in the distance
burst into flames.

اعتراف

«به خواهرم»

همه این سال‌ها

من با چشم‌های تو گریه کردم

و تو با لب‌های من اعتراف کردی

ما هر دو نام یکدیگر را با دستانی که مال ما نبود

می‌نوشتیم

و بعد از آن باورمان شد

که باید تا مدت‌ها

فقط خواب همدیگر را ببینیم.

CONFESSION

To My Sister

For all these years
I have wept with your eyes
and you have confessed with my lips
both of us wrote each other's names with hands
that were not our own
and after that we believed
that for a long time we must see each other
only in one another's dreams.

⌐

مجسمه

بدون اینکه بخواهم
مجسمه‌ای از من ساختی،
چشم‌های مجسمه به جهان بسته بود،
جهان، پشتِ پنجره بود
فکر کردم
این مرگ است که در تنِ سنگ می‌دود؟
به تو نگاه کردم
که یک جفت چشمِ زنده بودی
در پسِ سنگ.
گفتم: نه!
خواستی خودم را به تو بسپارم
تا دنیا از حرکت بایستد
ایستاد
تو را بوسیدم
انقلابی در گرفت
مردم به خیابان‌ها ریختند
مجسمه‌ها را شکستند
از ما فقط ملافه‌های سفید با ردهایی به جا ماند
مثل کتیبه‌هایی با حروف میخی
که روی آن نوشته بود: موزه دروغ‌گوترین راوی تاریخ است.

STATUE

Without my wanting it
you made me into a statue,
the statue's eyes were closed to the world;
I thought
the world was behind a pane of glass.
I thought
is this death that runs through the stone's body?
I looked at you
you were a pair of living eyes
behind stone.
I said: No!
you wanted me to give myself to you
so that the world would stop;
it stopped.
I kissed you
a revolution erupted
people poured into the streets
they smashed the statues
and all that was left of us was white sheets
like inscriptions in cuneiform
and on them was written: The Museum of History's
    Most Untruthful Storyteller.

(۱) جیم مثل جنگ

کلاه خود نبودم

پوتین نبودم

خمپاره نبودم

تانک نبودم

من

فرمانده نبودم

سرباز نبودم

میدان مین،

سیم خاردار

خاکریز نبودم من

یک تکه عکس کوچک و بی‌گوشه بودم

در جیب سمت چپ، از بالا

روی خون گرمِ قلب متلاشی سرباز وظیفه.

W FOR WAR (1)

I
wasn't a helmet
I wasn't a boot
I wasn't a mortar-shell
I wasn't a tank

I
wasn't a commander
I wasn't a soldier
a minefield
barbed wire
an embankment, not me
I was a bit of a photograph, small, with no corners
in the left-hand breast pocket
over the smashed heart of a conscript.

⌒

(۲) جیم مثل جنگ

گذشته‌ام
مثل سربازی شکسته‌خورده
از جنگی طولانی
با یک دست
برمی‌گردد
و در می‌زند
از هشتی، بی‌صدا
نگاه می‌کنم
نه!
دیگر نمی‌شناسمش
سرباز به سمت در خروجی
بر می‌گردد
آستین خالی‌اش را بالا می‌آورد
اشک‌هایش را پاک می‌کند
و بعد
آن را به لباسش
سنجاق می‌کند
و در ساختمان را پشت سرش
می‌بندد
و می‌رود
برای همیشه.

W FOR WAR (2)

My past
is like a wounded soldier
from a long war
who returns
with one arm
that knocks at the door –
from the hallway, without making a sound,
I watch him

No

I don't know him anymore
the soldier goes back
towards the exit
he lifts up his empty sleeve
wiping away his tears
and then
he pins it to his clothes
and closes the door of the building
behind him
and leaves
forever.

کاش

کاش خطی بنویسی و دلم باز شود
کاش اصلاً برسی از در و آغاز شود
عشق دیوانه کند باز مرا تا هر شب
از شراب تن تو شهر چو شیراز شود
مثل باغ ارمی، بوی بهار نارنج
از لبت سر زده، ای کاش لبت باز شود
چند روزیست که خاموش‌تر از خاموشم
هی به امید صدای تو که آواز شود
کاش می‌شد بنویسم که چه حالی . . . امّا
عشق بهتر که زمین خورده‌ی ایجاز شود
پشت این بیت زنی عاشق مردی شده است
تا به فرمان غزل پرده بر این راز شود
کاشکی شعر نیاید به زبانم دیگر
یا فقط عشق شما قافیه‌پرداز شود.

I WISH

I wish you'd write to me, and open up my heart,
I wish you'd come in through the door, and let things start

Love maddens me again, your body's wine each night
Had made this town Shiraz, a city of delight

You're like the Garden of Eram,* and fragrantly
Your lips breathe orange blossom; ah, open them for me!

How many days I've been more silent now than silence
Hoping to hear your voice approaching from the distance

I wish that I could write, say how it feels . . . however
When love has stumbled . . . if it's brief, so much the better

Behind this line a woman loves a man, a way
Poetic form keeps secret all she cannot say

I wish that no more poems would come, or that each time
They came to me your love would be their only rhyme.

———

---

* A legendary pre-Islamic garden said to be of great beauty,
also a historic Persian garden in Shiraz.

ماهی‌گیر

صیّاد،
تمام ِ شب تور می‌اندازد
و رویا می‌بافد
با ماهی‌های ناکام.
خواب با چشم می‌جنگد
سرما با تن
صیاد با آب
ماهی با هوا
و من با غریتی که سر گریختن ندارد.

FISHERMAN

The fisherman
all night he casts his net
and weaves dreams
with the fish that don't make it
sleep fights with the eyes
cold with the body
the fisherman with the water
the fish with the air
and I with exile, which is inescapable

در جستجوی وطن

از مرزها گذشته تنم، خانه‌ام کجاست؟
آن خنده‌های روشنِ دیوانه‌ام کجاست؟
از من گرفته‌اند تمامِ گذشته را
حتی نگفته‌اند که افسانه‌ام کجاست
در روزگارِ تلخ‌تر از زهرِ محتسب
از من نپرس جرعه و پیمانه‌ام کجاست
در غربت زمانه کبوتر شدن کم است
ای دام‌های فاصله، شادانه‌ام کجاست؟
از بادبادکی که هوا می‌رود بپرس
جغرافیای خسته‌یِ ویرانه‌ام کجاست؟
ای در سکوت و خلوتِ غربت شکستنی!
ای بغض بی‌بهانه! بگو شانه‌ام کجاست؟

IN SEARCH OF A HOMELAND

My body has crossed all borders, and my homeland . . .
  is where?
And those sunny, crazy smiles of mine . . . are where?

They took all of the past from me . . .
As for my dreams, they neglected to say where they are

In the time of the morals police, more bitter than poison,
The wine drops, the wine glass, don't ask me where they are

In exile the possibilities of becoming a dove are rare
O cages of distance . . . those millet seeds* fed to the doves . . .
  are where?

And question the kite that's riding the wind
Where my worn-out geography, my ruined homeland now are

Breaking in silence and the privacy of brittle exile,
O grudge with no excuse! And a shoulder to cry on . . .
  is where?

          ᴗ

---

* In Mashhad, there is an old tradition of feeding doves with millet
seeds. The memory of this is a very vivid one for natives of this city.

باتلاق

تنهایی! ای همیشه‌ترین اتّفاق من
آوازه‌خوان شهرِ شبِ بی‌چراغ من
تنهایی ای ترانه‌ی عزلت! شکوه درد!
بگذار سر به شانه‌ی چشمان داغ من
بگذار سر که با تو بگویم چگونه رفت
اردیبهشت سبز از این زردباغ من
حرفی نمانده روی دلم جز همین که نور
یخ بسته پشت پنجره‌های اتاق من
اندوه یک پرنده‌ی بی‌بال با من است
پروازِ مرگ آمده امشب سراغ من
شیرین‌ترین گناه جهان را به من بده
تلخ آمده‌ست طعم خدا بر مذاق من
اینجا درون من غزلی غرق می‌شود
مثل شکوه عشق تو در باتلاق من
این بار قصه‌ی من و خرداد تلخ بود
بی‌خانمان شد آخر قصه کلاغ من.

THE MARSH

To be alone! My commonest, my constant plight,
The singer in my city dark with lampless night

Alone! the song of my seclusion, and pain's blossom,
Lay your head against my shoulder here, my burning sight,

Lay your head, and I shall tell you how green May has gone
And left my garden now a withered yellow site

No words remain within my heart except to say
Behind my room's blank windows ice congeals the light

The sorrow of a wingless bird is with me now
It is the flight of death that tracks me down tonight

Give me the sweetest sin the world provides; the taste
Of God inside my mouth's become a bitter blight

Within me here love's poem drowns; it's like your love's
Sweet blossom sucked down in my marsh and out of sight

This time my story and that June were bitter; at last —
The crow of my story was homeless, and as black as night.

چیزهایی برای گفتن

این غصه‌ی بی‌انتها، گفتن ندارد که!
این گریه‌های بی‌صدا، گفتن ندارد که!

این شعرهای خسته و مغشوش و تکراری
این دردهای بی‌دوا، گفتن ندارد که!

این که دلم تنگ کسی بود و . . . هنوزم هست
یک حس بی‌آب و هوا، گفتن ندارد که!
شب، تیک‌تاک استخوان‌های نفس‌گیرت
شرح فضایی مرگزا، گفتن ندارد که!

وقتی که راهی جز گذشتن نیست، باور کن!
یک مشت حرفِ بی‌هجا، گفتن ندارد که!

نگذاشت این پاییز را هم عاشقش باشم
این تا ابد اسفندها، گفتن ندارد که!
سرد است، تخت و میز و بشقاب و . . .
زمین سرد است
تغییر محسوس دما گفتن ندارد که!
آقا! شما را دوست . . .

THINGS TO SAY

This endless unhappiness, there's nothing to say
These silent tears of distress, there's nothing to say

These poems, worn out, confused, repetitious,
Aches that are remediless, there's nothing to say

That I missed someone so much . . . and still do
A feeling of amorphousness, there's nothing to say

In the night, the heart-stopping creak of your bones
It's the nearness of death they express, there's nothing to say

When there's nowhere to go but away, believe me,
With a fistful of words that are substanceless, there's nothing
    to say

In the autumn he wouldn't let me love him still
It's February forever more or less, there's nothing to say

It's cold, the bed and table and plate and . . .
    the ground is cold
Not a breath of change nonetheless, there's nothing to say

Sir! I love . . . no! I can't anymore – I . . . you . . .
About our broken bodies I guess, there's nothing to say

نه!

دیگر ندارم من

من، تو . . . . شکس-تن‌های ما گفتن ندارد که!

سال هزار و سیصد و هشتاد و . . . . هر چه بود

تقویم‌های پر عزا، گفتن ندارد که!

سخت است رفتن، کندن از "جان" و "دل‌ت سخت است

آن گریه‌ها و شانه‌ها . . .

گفتن ندارد که!

دیگر نپرس از من کجا، کِی زندگی گم شد

یک مرگِ بی‌چون و چرا گفتن ندارد که!

The year was 1380 something* . . . whatever it was,
Mourning filled the diaries nevertheless, there's
   nothing to say

It's hard to leave, to tear up heart and soul, it's hard
Those tears, those shoulders, helplessness, there's
   nothing to say

Don't ask me where or when this life was lost, a death
   that has
No why or wherefore, that's meaningless, there's
   nothing to say.

⌐

---

* The year that this line refers to in the original Persian
poem is 1388, equivalent to 2009 in the Western calendar.
It is a reference to the post-election turmoil and the Green
uprising in 2009 in Iran following which the poet was forced
to live in exile up to the present (see Introduction, p. xiv).

خانه

اگرچه در خانه نیستم، ولی به جان دوست دارمش
میان آغوش هر بهار هنوز جا می‌گذارمش
شبیه رازی نگفتنیست، جنون ویرانِ غربتم
به دور از چشم عاقلان، به شعرها می‌سپارمش
گذشت عمری و روز و شب، شمرده‌ام ماه و سال را
به خواب و بیداری‌ام هنوز . . . . هنوز هم می‌شمارش
نخواه از من که بگذرم، نخواه تا دیگری شوم
نخواه برگشتن مرا به خانه‌ای که ندارمش
بهای گورکن اگر چه از بهای آیینه بیشتر
به دفن مردانِ کینه خواه، به دفن شب می‌گُمارمش
اگر نبینم دوباره باز، به عمر خود روی خانه را
به جان یک ابر می‌روم که تا همیشه ببارمش.

HOME

I'm not at home, but even so I love home in my soul,
I leave home in spring's arms each time that spring comes
    back again

The madness of my exile's like a secret left unsaid,
I place it in my poems far from glances of the sane

A life has passed, and day and night I count the months
    and years,
In sleep and in my waking still I count their old refrain

Don't say I ought to let it go, don't say I ought to change,
And now I have no home, don't say I should go back again

Though a gravedigger's price is more than a mirror's, I'll
    have*
The mirror bury the night and those men whose hatred's
    all too plain

If then, in all my life, I'll never see my home again
I'll creep into a cloud, and pour forever there as rain.

⌒

---

* The idea of the gravedigger's price has been borrowed from one of
the famous poems by Ahmad Shamlou: "I dread, however, to die in
a land where, the gravedigger's wages / Exceed the price of human
freedom."For more information see: https://iransnews.wordpress.
com/2014/07/29/ahmad-shamlou-poems-such-a-weird-time-it-is/.

جزیره

هی ذره ذره ذره دلم را مذاب کن
هی جرعه جرعه جرعه شبم را شراب کن
هی تکه تکه تکه بساز این شکسته را
با من برقص و زندگی‌ام را خراب کن
بگذار تا گناه " تو" را مرتکب شوم
اصلاً مرا نواده‌ی شیطان خطاب کن
از حرف‌های خسته‌ی یک مست پاپتی
شعری بساز و دور گلویم طناب کن
زندان حصر من غزل دست‌های توست
تسخیر کن، محاصره کن، انقلاب کن
در من جزیره‌ای‌ست که متروک مانده است
پهلو بگیر در دل من اعتصاب کن
اینجا هوای حادثه ابری‌ست خوب من
بگذر از این جزیره کمی آفتاب کن
افتاده جام از لب این لحظه‌های مست
فکری به حال خلسه‌ی بعد از شراب کن.

ISLAND

Oh bit by bit by bit, dissolve this heart of mine
Oh drop by drop by drop resolve my night in wine

I'm broken, piece by piece by piece refashion me
And dance with me, and oh destroy my life for me

Go on, till you're the evil that I'm guilty of,
And say that I'm the devil's grand-daughter, my love

With a barefoot drunkard's words worn out from use
Write verses, place them round my neck now as a noose

My fortress-prison is the poem your hands make –
Seize it, besiege it, overthrow it for my sake

There is an island in me, abandoned and apart,
Land there . . . provoke an insurrection in my heart

The clouds hide everything that happens there, my love
Shine there . . . send down a little sunlight from above

The wine glass slips from our lips, the drunken moments
   pass
Think of our pleasure once we've set aside this glass.

فصل جنون

با چشم‌های قهوه‌ای‌ات باز رد شدی
راه خراب کردن ما را بلد شدی
شب بود و دست‌های تو از نور ماه پر
شکل ستاره‌ای که رصد می‌شود شدی
گم شد دوباره این دل بی‌صاحبم چه زود
مثل تبی که در تن من می‌دود شدی
دارم به مرتکب شدنت فکر می‌کنم
مرز میان حادثه‌ی خوب و بد شدی
زیر نگاه تو، دل من تکه‌تکه‌تر
تک‌تازیانه‌های نفس‌گیر حد شدی
اجرای حکم با تو که درعمق جان من
محکوم ماندگاری و حبس ابد شدی
پیچید بوی خوب تو در شعرهای من
وقتی برای فصل جنون نامزد شدی.

THE SEASON OF MADNESS

Again, with your brown eyes, you passed right by me
You're well aware of how you can destroy me

It was night, your hands were full of moonlight
As if you were a star observed by me

How quickly my ungoverned heart is lost again
And you've become a fever running fast in me

I think of sinning by my love, and you're
The line that marks off wrong from right for me

Beneath your gaze my heart was shattered . . . you're
The gasps, the whip-strokes meted out to me

You execute this sentence, though you're now
A prisoner of my soul's depths, chained in me

Your sweet scent tangled in my poems that time
I named you as the madness lodged in me.

آفرینش

با شعر و شور و آتش و شب آفریدمت
با لحظه‌های مستی و تب آفریدمت
با دست‌های خالی و با جام‌های پر
با جان خود وجب به وجب آفریدمت
آن اسم اعظمی تو که بی‌وقفه آشناست
مثل خدا، بدون لقب آفریدمت
آنجا که آفتاب به شب طعنه می‌زند
با خاک توس و تار و طرب آفریدمت
مجنون لهجه‌دار خراسانی‌ات شدم
با طعم خوب بوسه و لب آفریدمت
شب آمدی، سکوت و کویرم ستاره داد
بی‌واژه و بدون سبب آفریدمت.

CREATION

With poetry and passion, with fire and night,
I created you
With moments of drunkenness, with feverish delight,
I created you

With empty hands, with glasses filled with wine,
Inch by inch, and with my own soul's light,
I created you

Your marvelous name's known always, everywhere,
Like God Himself, without a title and outright,
I created you

With soil from Tus,* with music and with joy,
There, where the sun reproves the night,
I created you

I became your beloved, with my Khorasani accent,
With the sweet taste of kisses, as our lips unite,
I created you

Silent, you came at night, my desert filled with stars,
For no reason at all, with no words I can write,
I created you.

　　　　　﹏

---

* Tus is an ancient city near Mashhad in Khorasan, Iran.
The revered tenth-century Persian poet Abolqasem Ferdowsi,
author of *The Shahnameh,* was born there.

یواشکی

بوسیدمش کنار خیابان، یواشکی

دور از نگاه گزمه و ستوان، یواشکی

گم می‌شدیم در تن هم، چشم‌های هم

با دست‌های در هم و لرزان، یواشکی

می ریخت عشقمان به تن کوچه‌ها شراب

کتمان دین و باور و ایمان، یواشکی

چادرسیاه ِ شب‌زده‌ی روزهای دور

در کیف‌های مدرسه پنهان، یواشکی

هر روز با دو چهره‌ی همواره مختلف

از گشت های مرگ، گریزان، یواشکی

در حسرت رهایی تعزیرناپذیر

ای کاش می‌رسید به پایان یواشکی.

STEALTHILY

I kissed him by the side of the road, stealthily
Out of the officer's, the night-watch's, sight, stealthily
We were lost in one another's bodies and eyes
Our hands twined together and trembling, stealthily
Our love dripped wine on the alley's body
On religion's scruples, on faith and belief, stealthily
The black veil of night, and far-off days,
The thrills in school, in secret, stealthily
Every day, always, with two faces
Fleeing from Death's patrols, stealthily
Longing to be free of unwelcome condemnation
How I wish it could come to an end, stealthily.

مسافر

سفر می‌کنم در تنت، مست، هر شب

در آغوش بیهوش غرقِ تو در تب

در آن شانه‌های به آتش نشسته

دهانِ پر از بوسه‌های مُحدّب

جهانم همین تخت باشد، همین تن

همین گونه‌ها با خطوط مُورأب

بگیران مرا با سرانگشت‌هایت

به کامی، به جامی که تا پاسی از شب،

برقصانمت مست در دست‌هایم

بشعرانمت با ردیفِ: مُرکّب

من آن اسب رویین‌تن خوش‌رکابم

تو تازنده با شعرهایی که بر لب . . .

همین لحظه ای کاش زهرت بریزد

به جانم که می‌پیچد از نیش عقرب

نماند به جا از تو، از من، قراری

که با بی‌قراری، تو را مست . . . هر شب . . .

TRAVELER

Each night, I travel in your body, feverish,
Drunk, drowned, effaced in your embrace

Held by you, seated on fire, my mouth
Holds the curve of your kisses in place

My world is this bed, this body,
The lines that define the shape of your face

Now let your fingertips excite me
And drunkenly delight me, as night moves on apace

Within my hands I'll make you drunk, I'll make you dance,
I'll make of you a poem with all its rhymes in place

And I'm that bronze horse, proud, high-stepping, that you ride
With poems on your lips, urged on now at a furious pace

Would that at this moment you'd dart your poison into me –
A scorpion stings my writhing soul in its embrace

There is no rest for either you or me . . . each night now,
Drunk on you, no rest in any place.

⌒

حتی اگر هرگز نباشی

می‌خواهمت در لحظه‌های بی‌قراری
در خواب و بیداری و این شب زنده‌داری
می‌خواهمت در روزهای سرد و خاموش
در اوج این بیهودگی، بیهوده‌کاری
می‌خواهمت در فصل فصل زنده بودن
در روزهای برفی و گرم و بهاری
می‌خواهمت، می‌خواهمت، هر لحظه، هر روز
می‌خواهمت ای خونِ در رگ‌هام جاری!
می‌خواهمت حتی اگر هرگز نباشی
حتی اگر کاری به احساسم نداری
می‌خواهمت از دور از نزدیک، هر جا
هر جا که هستی با تمام هر چه داری.

EVEN IF YOU'RE NEVER TO BE HERE

I want you in my moments of uncertainty,
Asleep, awake, and in this night of watching endlessly
I want you on cold silent days, I want you in
This wave of pointlessness, this vain futility
I want you season after season in my life
On snowy days, hot days, and spring's vitality
I want you, I want you every moment of each day
Oh blood that flows within my every artery
I want you even if you're never to be here
And even if you never give a thought to me
I want you from afar, from near, from everywhere
With all you have and are, wherever you may be.

پالتو

لعنت به پالتوی خاکستری‌ات
که همزمان
بوی تن و
هوس خواستن و
داغ عطر نایاب و گران آن شرکت ورشکست شده کذایی را
با هم به دلم می‌ریزد.
لعنت به پالتوی خاکستری‌ات
و نه خودت.

OVERCOAT

I curse your gray overcoat
that all at once pours
the smell of your body
and of wanting you,
and the rare expensive scent produced
by that damned company that's bankrupt now
into my heart
I curse your gray overcoat
not you.

⌒

گوهردشت

«به کیوان صمیمی بهبهانی»

می‌پرسم از خودم که تو آنجا چه می‌کنی
این روزهای مرده و این سال‌های سرد
با آن صدای گرم، چه تقسیم می‌کنی؟
یک قرص نان و چند قلم شعر یا سرود
یا خاطرات روشن آن روزهای دور
تا رشته امید ز هم نگلسد به جور
از پشت این دریچه‌ی خاموش، ناگهان
با هر چه سخت‌جانی و با هر چه خستگی
نامت بر این بسیط نفس‌گیر مرگزای
آغاز راه گمشده جاودانگی‌ست
از رد پای سرخ تو بر پهن‌دشت برف
گل می‌دهد چکامه و شعری که زندگی‌ست.

GOWHARDASHT[*]

To Keyvan Samimi Behbehani

I ask myself what you are doing there
in these dead days, in these cold years,
with your warm voice, what is it that you share?
a round of flat bread, and a few poems or songs,
or bright memories of those far-off days
so that hope's thread isn't forced to unravel . . .
from behind this silent trap-door, suddenly,
in spite of my heart's endurance, my weariness,
your name, in this place of blocked breath
that generates death, is the start of a lost eternal road . . .
in your red footprints on a snow-covered plain
the songs and poems that are life will blossom.

---

[*] Gowhardasht is the name of a prison in the vicinity of Karaj,
near the capital city of Tehran, where prisoners of conscience
are kept. Keyvan Samimi Behbahani, editor for many years of
the reformist journal *Nameh*, was one of the most influential and
well-known political prisoners there. The author knew him and
his children personally and dedicated this poem to his children
when he was in imprisoned after the 2009 post-election turmoil.

محبوس

تو نیستی و دلم ذره ذره سنگ شده
تمام زندگی‌ام بغض یک نهنگ شده
نشسته‌ام کف دریای لعنتی و دلم
برای دیدن و بوسیدن تو تنگ شده
بـدون ایـنکه بـخواهـم، تـفنگ تـنهایی
دوباره، از تو چه پنهان، پر از فشنگ شده
گلوله پشت گلوله، بدون آتش‌بس
تو نیستی و غزل، شعرِ تلخِ جنگ شده
نمی‌رسیم به هـم، کوچه‌ی تو بن‌بست است
دلم بدون تو یک مادیان لنگ شده
تو قرص ماهی و در جزر و مد خواستنات
دو دست عاشق من پنجه‌ی پلنگ شده
چقدر قصه بگویم؟ چرا نمی‌فهمی؟
دلم برای تو بی‌استعاره تنگ شده

BLOCKED OFF

You're not here now, and bit by bit my heart's become
  a stone;
And into a sea-monster my whole life's grief has grown –
I'm sitting on this sea-bed, I curse it and I miss you
My heart is filled with longing now to see you and to kiss
  you
Without my wanting it the rifle loneliness has been
  provided
With bullets, and it's loaded – from you why should I hide
  it? –
With bullet after bullet, with no cease-fire anymore,
You're absent, and my love song's now a bitter song of war
We cannot reach each other, your road's blocked off, not
  there,
Without you here my heart's become a lamely limping
  mare
You are the moon's disc, and the tide of wanting you now
  draws
Me forward and my loving hands become a leopard's claws.
But how much must I tell you? Why don't you comprehend
That really, with no metaphors, I miss you without end.

پیاده

از من دو چشم و یک دل ناسور مانده است
یک دل، دلی که از همه جا دور مانده است
از من همین دو پای پیاده به سمت هیچ
یک مشت خاک و یک تنِ بی‌گور مانده است
غربت، شروع خسته‌ی پایان زندگی‌ست
این درد، سال‌هاست که مهجور مانده است
حجم کتاب و خاطره و شعر و سررسید
از مادرم سه عکس و کمی . . . نور مانده است
اینجا در این ترانه، کسی جان سپرده است
دیوانه‌ای که از وطنش دور مانده است.

ON FOOT

Of me two eyes now and one heart in pain remain
exiled from everywhere, that can't go back again
I'm going now on foot to nothingness . . . one fist
of dirt, one body no grave can contain, remain
exiled, the weary start of what is left of life,
the years of this excluded, solitary pain, remain
a pile of books, and memories, and poems, and from
my mother, three pictures and a little . . . light remain
here, in this song, someone has given up the ghost
insane, she can't go home again, and must remain.

جنین

خون می‌چکد، کودک درون چاه می‌افتد
امشب زنی از نردبان ماه می‌افتد
خون می‌چکد، از لحظه‌های چرک این غربت
از عشق، از دلواپسی، از خشم، از شهوت
خون می‌چکد از بغض‌های مرده در گوشی
از لحظه‌های سرد و خاموش هم‌آغوشی
از قاب عکس تو که پشتش نیستی دیگر
از خاطرات من، از این آوار خاکستر
از من که دردم می‌کند دیوانه‌تر هر روز
از زخم‌های کهنه‌ی این سال آدم‌سوز
کودک درون خون من، آرام می‌گیرد
امشب درون چاه می‌افتد، و می‌میرد
کودک تمام زندگی، کودک دل من بود
آن لخته‌های خون شبیه روح یک زن بود
ای کاش از خون خودم، یک جرعه می‌خوردم
امشب کنار کودکم، آرام می‌مردم.

THE FETUS

Blood drips, the child falls in the well; tonight
A woman falls from the ladder of moonlight
Blood drips from exile's filthy moments here
From love, from lust, from anger, anxious fear
Blood drips, from pent-up sorrow that has died,
From cold and silent moments side by side
From your picture's frame from which you've gone
From my memories, and from this ashen song
From me whose pain each day feeds my mad yearning
From old wounds, from this year of human burning
The child within my blood, how calm she lies.
Tonight she falls into the well and dies,
The child of all my life, my heart; blood-smeared,
And from these smears a woman's ghost appeared.
Would that I'd drunk my blood, one drop; beside
My child, tonight, at peace, I would have died.

اندوه خاموش

ترسیدم از خوابی که می‌بلعید بالم را
دیوانه‌بازی‌های خوب پارسالم را
ترسیدم از تن‌تکه‌های آشنایی که
فریاد می‌زد با صدای مرده فالم را
یک شاعر تنهای تبعیدی که می‌رقصید
با بیت‌های خسته‌اش اندوه لالم را
من بال بالِ مردنم را می‌زدم وقتی
صاحب قفس با عشق می‌پرسید حالم را
بیست و . . .
کمی هم بیشتر . . .
ماه است
یا خورشید؟
گم کرده‌ام تاریخ آغاز زوالم را
شنبه، دوشنبه، چهارشنبه، جمعه، فرقش چیست؟
وقتی زمان پس می‌زند روز وصالم را
پاییز هم دست از سر ما بر نمی‌دارد
ای کاش تنهایی شبی می‌کَند قالم را
از من کسی برگشت دیشب، بی‌خداحافظ
از من کسی برگشت دیشب
بی‌خداحافظ
از من کسی
برگشت
دیشب
بی‌خداحافظ
برگشت تا ممکن کند مرگِ محالم را.

SILENT SORROW

I feared my dream, the one that swallowed down
  my wings,
My last year's passionate antics, love-crazy things,
I feared the hacked-in-pieces flesh of one I knew
Whose dead voice cried aloud the fate I would
  live through –
A poet alone, in exile, dancing restlessly
Through my silent sorrow, with her weary poetry –
When kindly the cage keeper asked how I was doing
My lonely wings were flapping wildly, I was dying
Twenty-somethingth of the month, or sun, or more ago?
The date of when my downfall started . . . I don't know
Saturday, Wednesday, Friday, what's the difference when
Time takes away the day I was in love again
Even the autumn won't allow me to go free –
Would that one night my loneliness might slaughter me .
  . .

And someone left me here last night, with no Goodbye,
To make it possible at last for me to die.

به رنگ آتش

از تمام جهان
تنها صدای قلب یک زن را می‌شنوم
که در نوزده سالگی
کتاب سمفونی مردگان را
سه بار در یک سال خوانده است
و فیلم «به رنگ آتش» را دوست دارد
دهانش را می‌بوسم
مثل قرص‌های ضربان‌اش
یکی صبح، یکی عصر
پشت پرده‌های زرد ضخیم
باد می‌آید
سینه‌ی چپش را در مشتم می‌گیرم
سال تمام می‌شود
من از تمام جهان بیرونم.

THE COLOR OF FIRE

From all the world
I hear only the beating of one woman's heart
who at the age of nineteen
has read the novel "*Symphony of the Dead*"
three times in one year
and loves the film "*The Color of Fire*"
I kiss her mouth
like the pills for her heart beat
one in the morning, one in the evening
behind thick yellow curtains
the wind comes
I take her left breast in my hand
the year ends
I am outside of the whole world.

حقیقت

حقیقت آن است

که من روزی می‌میرم

و دیگر کسی نیست لای این روزنامه‌ها

لای این فیش‌های برق و آب

برای یافتن نشانی از تو

بی آنکه بدانی

روزی سه مرتبه کاغذها را زیر و رو کند.

من به مرگ خودم فکر نمی‌کنم

به تو فکر می‌کنم.

که آن روز،

بدون داشتن یکی مثل من

در این دنیا

چقدر تنها خواهی ماند.

TRUTH

The truth is
that one day I'll die
and then no one will go through these newspapers,
through these electricity and water bills,
shuffling papers three times a day
to find some sign of you
without your knowing it.
I'm not thinking of my death
I'm thinking of you
and how that day
without having someone like me in the world
how lonely you will be.

بیگانه

من، عاشق مردانی بودم
که هرگز نمی‌شناختم
شعرهایم، همه در وصف عابران پیاده‌ای بود
که تنها، در باران می‌گذشتند
با بارانی‌هایی که بوی بلوط سوخته می‌دادند.
من، عاشق مردانی بودم
که همیشه جوان می‌مردند
خیلی جوان.
چشم‌هایشان، در واپسین لحظات،
ناگهان، خاکستری می‌شد.
آن‌ها،
هیچ‌کدام،
هیچ‌وقت
لب نداشتند
و آغوش‌شان،
شبیه مکعب‌های مغشوش و گیج
با تصویر هیچ زنی آرام نمی‌شد.

STRANGER

I was in love with men
whom I never knew
My poems were always about men who walked by me,
who passed by alone, in the rain,
the rain that gave off a smell of burned acorns.
I was in love with men
who always died young,
very young.
Their eyes, in their last moments,
would suddenly become ashen.
These men,
none of them,
ever,
had lips
and their chests
were like misshapen twisted cubes
that no woman's image could bring peace to.

ᴗᴗ

صدف‌ها

رازهای خیابان را

مثل صدف

در جیب‌هایم ریختم

از چهارراه گذشتم

ته هر کوچه‌ی سالخورده

دریایی پیدا بود.

SHELLS

The roads' secrets,
like shells,
I've slipped them in my pockets
I've passed the crossroads
At the end of every ancient alleyway
a sea was visible.

بهاریه ۴۹

پنج سال و کمی بیشتر، پر
عشق پر، خانه پر، شور و شر پر
رفته بودم که برگردم اما
ناگهان جاده‌ی پشت سر پر
رنگ تبعید، خاکستری بود
خنده‌های سپید پدر پر
سال‌ها رفت و بر جا دلی ماند
سرد، سرخورده دلتنگ، پرپر
کاشکی، کاش برگشتنی بود
آرزو، کاش، اما، اگر، پر
ماندم و باز از سر گرفتم
عشقِ بیهوده‌ی بی‌ثمر پر
روزهای دروغ و تظاهر
لافِ پوچ قضا و قدر پر
امن، عاشق، رها، خانه اینجاست
روزهایِ بدِ در به در پر.

SPRING '94[*]

It's been five years, a little more now, flown away –
Of love, of home, of happiness, all flown away
I left intending to return, but then
The road behind me, suddenly, had flown away
The color of my exile was like ash
The white smiles of my father, flown away
The years went by, a heart remained behind,
Cold, disillusioned, homesick . . . flown away.
Would that . . . I wish I could go back again
Wishing, wanting, but and if . . . all flown away
I stayed, and once again I started out
The useless love that leads to nowhere, flown away
The days of lies and of hypocrisy
The empty boasts of Fate and Destiny, flown away
Safe now, in love, and free, my home is here –
The bad days of my homelessness . . . have flown away.

⌒

---

[*] In the Persian solar calendar, 1394 is equivalent to 2015 in the
Western calendar. Writing poems upon the arrival of the spring
is a tradition that goes back a long way in Persian literature, one
that is maintained by contemporary poets.

غزل رفتن

یک نفر رفت که از دست خودش گم شود و
راحت از شر رجزخوانی مردم شود و
یک نفر رفت و می‌خواست که حرفی نزند
خالی از حس نفس‌گیر تکلم شود و
یک نفر با همه بیگانه و از خود بیزار
در پی آتش و ویرانه، که کژدُم شود و
شیر انداخت و خط بین خود و سایه خویش
تا کدام آخر سر آتش هیزم شود و
رفت، آرام لباش را به لب باران داد
تا مگر ابر شود، غرق توهم شود و
پر بگیرد، برود سمت خراسان بزرگ
یک کبوتر وسط کوچه هشتم شود و
بال بر بال، در آغوش عزیز خورشید
صاحب صحن پر از ارزن و گندم شود و
یک نفر رفت، که رفت از همه جا تا شاید
یا فراموش و یا غرق و یا گم شود و . . .

LEAVING

Someone left, to lose herself, she went,
And to be free of gossips' harassment
She went and wanted to be silent, empty
Of the need to spell out what she meant,
And stranger now to everyone and sick
Of who she was, sought ruin, fire, intent
On being a scorpion, tossed the coin to see
Between her shadow and herself in its descent
Which finally would be a heap of sticks ablaze
She gently gave her lips then to the rain's lips, went
To see if she could be a cloud, lost in herself,
Take wing and fly to Khorasan's wide firmament
A dove aloft above Eighth Street,* her wings
Within the dear sun's arms, and their extent
Spread above wheat and millet in a courtyard
Someone left, left everywhere, so that perhaps
She'd be forgotten, lost, drowned, absent.

⌣

---

* A reference to the shrine of the eighth Shia Imam
which is located in Mashhad and is one of the most
important landmarks of the city. Also a reference to the
courtyards of the shrine, which are often filled with doves
(*see also* note on p. 33).

از آن روزها

زمین وحشت و تعلیق و اضطراب و خطر
زمین شاید و اما و احتمال و اگر
زمین دودی و خاکستری، زمینِ فشنگ
زمین رفتن و هرگز نیامدن دیگر

به سقفهای فشرده به دارهای حقیر
به اعتراف، به سیلی، به لحظهی تحقیر
به دست و پا زدن و مرگهای معمولی
به روزهای سیاهی که می‌شود تکثیر

نخواست دامنهی درد را ادامه دهد
سقوط یک بدن سرد را ادامه دهد
اگرچه خالی و خسته، اگرچه تلخ و اسیر
نخواست گریهی یک مرد را ادامه دهد

به زنده بودن خود توی آینه شک کرد
به روز مُردن خود توی آینه شک کرد
به «روز خوب» می‌آید، به دوستت دارم
به دل سپردن خود توی آینه شک کرد

نوشت آخرِ خط جای ایستادن نیست
گلوی باغ گرفته‌ست و نایِ خواندن نیست
نوشت و توی سرش هی مچاله شد، خفه شد
و فکر کرد زمین جای زنده ماندن نیست.

FROM THOSE DAYS

A land of terror, danger, worry, who knows when
A land of might be, but and if, of maybe then
A land of smoke and ash, a bullet-riddled land,
A land of leaving, never to return again

With crushing ceilings, gallows slight, despicable,
With slaps, confessions, times when you're contemptible,
With desperate struggling, and with death grown commonplace,
With days of darkness thickening, descending over all

She didn't want the aching to go on any more
Cold flesh disintegrating to go on any more
Though she was tired and empty, bitter and a prisoner,
She didn't want the weeping to go on any more

The mirror showed that she was there, she doubted it
The day when her own death was there, she doubted it,
And that "A good day will arrive" or "I love you,"
And even when she fell in love, she doubted it.

She wrote at the line's end, "There's no good place to stand,
The garden's throat is throttled, the flute-song's banned . . ."
She wrote, and in her head she crumpled and was silent
And thought, "There's nowhere left to live now, in this land."

تا که در آغوشت

فرزند جنگ بودم و چون تیری، هر سو روانه، تا که در آغوشت

رزمنده‌ای اسیر به دنبال یک آشیانه، تا که در آغوشت

آتش گرفته بود و نمی‌بارید باران بر آن زمین پر از کینه
می‌خواندمت تمام شب و هر روز مثل ترانه تا که در آغوشت

من بی‌قرار مرگ خودم بودم، در واقعیتی که فقط رویاست
رویای بی‌قراری و آتش‌بس، رویای خانه، تا که در آغوشت

پوتین، برای جنگ و برای صلح، پوتین، برای تا تو دویدن‌ها
پوتین، شهید راه دو پای لُخت، در آستانه، تا که در آغوشت

ای کاش راه امن فراری بود، از جنگ و این شکستن بی‌پایان
از بغض‌های ساکت بی‌شانه، از این شبانه، تا که در آغوشت

من خواب دیده‌ام که نمی‌میرم، در سنگریز خاطره می‌مانم
تا جنگ را دوباره بمیرانم تا بی‌بهانه، تا که در آغوشت.

UNTIL I'M IN YOUR ARMS

I was a child of war and like an arrow, speeding everywhere
                              until I'm in your arms

A captive struggling, fighting, looking for a nest somewhere,
                              until I'm in your arms

It was on fire, and no rain fell upon that land so filled with
   hatred
I called for you all night and every day, as if singing in despair
                     until I'm in your arms

I feared for my own death, that was in fact a dream, no more,
An anxious dream, of cease-fire and of home, a castle in the
   air,   until I'm in your arms

Boots for war and boots for peace, boots for running after you
Boots that saw the road two bare feet took, boots on the
   threshold there   until I'm in your arms

Would that there was a road to run away, be safe from war,
This endless ruin, these nightly silent sorrows I can't share
                              until I'm in your arms

I dreamed that I won't die, I'll stay within the scree of memory
Until I kill this war again, until - with no excuses there –
                              I'm in your arms.

تعقیب

عکس‌ها دروغ نمی‌گویند
من پیر شده‌ام
و عشق بیست‌سالگی‌ام را فراموش کرده‌ام
تو دیر کرده‌ای
کاغذ گران شده است
پستچی‌ها افسرده‌اند
هواپیماها بیشتر می‌افتند
و هیچ پرونده‌ای دیگر مختومه نمی‌شود.

PROSECUTION

Pictures don't lie
I've grown old
and I've forgotten the love I felt when I was twenty
you've come too late
paper's grown expensive
postmen have had enough
planes mostly crash
and no one else's file will ever be closed.

دوزیست

دوباره مرگ، دوباره زوال و نیست شدن
دوباره مثل وزغ خسته و دو زیست شدن
دوزیست یعنی در سراب جان دادن
به خواب، یک بدن مرده را تکان دادن
دو زیست یعنی اینجا کم است یک چیزی
میان خاطره‌ها مبهم است یک چیزی
دو زیست یعنی آنجا شبیه یک دریاست
کویر، فاجعه‌ی بیکران ماهی‌هاست
دو زیست یعنی: مردم! نفس کم آوردم
غزل کم آوردم، هم‌قفس کم آوردم
شبیه آدم برفی، شبیه بستنیِ
شبیه رابطه‌های کج گسستنیِ
شبیه حلقه‌ی زنجیرهای پاره شده
شبیه شعر بزک کرده استعاره شده
شبیه لحظه پرواز و بغض یک چمدان
شبیه حسرتِ پروازِ تا ابد تهران
دو زیست شد دل من تا نمیرد از دوری
شبیه خاطره‌ی سرد سنگ بر گوری.

AMPHIBIOUS

Once again death, once again fading to nothingness
Once again, like an exhausted frog, amphibious

Amphibious, which means dying in a mirage's gleam
And shaking a dead body within a dream

Amphibious, which means that something's missing here,
Among vague memories there's something that's not clear

Amphibious, which means that over there is like a sea,
A desert, for the fish a limitless calamity

Like a snowman, like an ice-cream disappearing
Like wrong relationships unraveling

Like a link from broken chains, or
Like a tawdry poem's metaphor

Like the moment of take-off and a suitcase's grieving
Like endless regret for Tehran that you're leaving

In exile my heart's become amphibious to survive
Like the cold memory of a stone that marks a grave.

⌒

غزه

خانه دروغ بزرگیست
دستت را به من بده
تا سه بشمار
و بدو
فراموش کن خانه را
در حافظه‌ات آوارش کن
موشکی بساز
و با دست خودت پرتابش کن به حافظه‌ات
باور کن، خانه دروغی بیش نیست
و تا مرگ تنها ده دقیقه فاصله است
دستت را به من بده
تا سه بشمار
چمدان و عکسها و عروسکها
گلدانها و ظرفها و صندلی‌ها
فراموششان کن
ملافه‌ها، ملافه‌های سفید را فقط بردار
با ته مانده‌های اکسیژن
نفس عمیق
برگرد،
پشته‌ای خاک را تصور کن

GAZA

Home is a big lie
give me your hand
count to three
and run
forget home
destroy it in your memory
make a missile
and launch it with your own hands against your memory
believe me, home is nothing more than a lie
and a death alone is only ten minutes away
give me your hand
count to three
suitcase and photographs and dolls
vases and plates and chairs
forget them all
take only sheets, white sheets
take a deep breath
of the little oxygen
that's left
now, turn back!
imagine a heap of dirt

آواری بر دستهای کاموایی عروسکت

حالا تنها دو دقیقه مانده است

می‌بینی مرگ چطور مثل حشره‌ای سمج در خیالمان

می‌دود؟

و خودش را به شیشه می‌کوبد؟

می‌افتد، پای پنجره، بی‌جان

و دوباره درست وقتی داریم می‌دویم

بلند می شود، خودش را به پنجره می‌کوبد

شیشه‌ها فرو می‌ریزند

و می‌افتد پای پنجره

رفته‌ایم و مرگ در خانه ما خودکشی می‌کند.

piled on your doll's knitted arms

now there are only two minutes left

can you see how death runs in our dreams like a
   nagging insect

and hurls itself against the window?

it falls lifeless at the foot of the window

and as we're running

it gets up again unhurt, and hurls itself against
   the window

the glass shatters

and it falls at the foot of the window.

we've left and death kills itself in our house.

فشنگ سرگردان

مثل فشنگی سرگردان و سمج
بازمانده از سال‌های دور
در خونم راه می‌رود
غربت.

WANDERING BULLET

It's like a wandering, nagging bullet
still there after many years
traveling in my blood,
exile.

اسیدپاشی

کاش می‌شد صورتم را بردارم
بگذارم جای صورت سوخته‌ات
و بعد باز آینه را برای همیشه
سمت تو بچرخانم.

ACID-THROWING

How I wish it were possible that I could remove my
    face
and put it in place of your burned face
and then forever turn a mirror
toward you.

⌒

جیم مثل جنگ (۳)

برای عزیز و کودکان جنگ در کوبانی

جنگ بود و گلوله می‌بارید
زنده ماندن چه کار سختی بود
هر طرف را نگاه می‌کردند
مرگ و آوار و تیره‌بختی بود

باید از خانه بار می‌بستند
سمت تاریک ناکجاآباد
سمت جغرافیای نامعلوم
سمت هر جا و هر چه باداباد

پشت سر خانه‌ای که گم می‌شد
در غبار سیاه و خاکستر
پیش رو، راه سخت و ناهموار
سیل آوارگان بی‌سنگر

شانه‌هایش پناه کودک بود
کودک دیگری در آغوشش
سومی می‌دوید از پی مرد
تلی از خاک بود تن‌پوشش

مادر از پی روانه و خاموش
کوهی از بغض و بی‌قراری بود
چشم در چشم جنگ و از چشمش
آب سرخ انار جاری بود

W FOR WAR (3)

In memory of Aziz
and children of war in Kobané

How hard it was to stay alive
In the war, the bullets' rain,
When everywhere they looked
Were death and darkness and pain

They had to pack and leave
And travel to who-knows-where
To a geography unknown,
That was anywhere but there

Behind them their lost home
Was black with ash, ahead
A hard uneven road
And the flood of those who fled

His shoulders carried a child
His arms were around another,
Behind them ran a third
Like a mound that dust-clouds smother

Their mother was following them,
A mountain of silence and dread,
Eye to eye with the war, tears flowed
Like pomegranate juice, blood-red.

آه، اما چه جنگ، وحشی بود
چنگ می‌زد به روی امیدش
دزد شادی کودکانش بود
با شکرخند خشم و تهدیدش

از سه کودک یکی نمی‌خندید
از سه کودک یکی پر از تب بود
بی‌وطن، بی‌صدا و بی آهنگ
مثل یک شعر بی‌مخاطب بود

باز مانده کنار راهی دور
خیره در مهربانی خورشید
تا که شاید یکی رسد از راه
تا که شاید یکی هم او را دید

جنگ آمد به هیئت آدم
مرگ آمد به قامت خورشید
چشم‌هایش در آسمان یخ زد
و دگر تا همیشه هیچ ندید

و دگر تا همیشه هیچ ندید
و دگر تا همیشه هیچ نگفت
چشم‌هایِ عزیزِ نازش را
بست آرام بر جنایت و خُفت.

Ah, but the war was brutal
Destroying her hopes with fear,
Stealing her children's joy
With its thuggish, violent sneer.

Three children – one didn't smile,
Three children – one had a fever,
They were homeless and silent now
Like a poem unheard forever

By the side of the road, bewildered
By the kindness of the sun,
Perhaps someone would come
And see him there, someone . . .

War came in the shape of a man,
Death came in the form of the sun
His eyes were fixed on the sky, frozen
Forever, and seeing no one

And then he saw nothing forever,
And forever now he kept
His silence, and closed his infant eyes
On the crimes around him, and slept.

⌣

شعری برای ایران

خس خس درون سینه‌ام یاد تو می‌میرد
دل بی‌نهایت نیست، گاهی سخت می‌گیرد

خس‌خس درون سرفه‌های کهنه‌ام، هر شب
هم‌بسترم: کابوس یا هذیانِ بعد از تب

هر شب شبیه سایه‌ای بر سقف یا دیوار
می‌بینمت، در خواب و بیداری، به استمرار

دست از سرم، دست از وجودم برنمی‌داری
هر شب فقط در خواب‌هایم درد می‌کاری

یک مشت خاکی، دور و زخمی و زمستانی
دلتنگ آن یک مشت خاکم، تو نمی‌دانی!

یک بیکران دریای خاموشی پر از ماهی
یک مشت بغض ناگهان، یک آسمان آهی

مثل کلاس درس و یاران دبستانی
یا این پرستوهای وقت کوچ می‌مانی

تو باند پروازی که بالت را درو کردند
بعد از سقوطت، لاشخورها، بال، نو کردند

A POEM FOR IRAN

Bit by bit now, in my breast, your memory dies from me
The heart's not infinite, and sometimes sorrow seizes me

Bit by bit now, every night, within my ancient coughs
A nightmare shares my pillow, and leaves me fevered, or
    delirious

On the wall or on the ceiling, you're like a shadow that I see
Each night, whether I sleep or lie awake, incessantly

You won't release my being, you won't release my brain
And each night in my dreams you sow there only pain

You're a fistful of dirt, wounded, a winter, a distant land,
How much I miss that fistful you'll never understand!

A shoreless, silent, fish-filled sea, and in another guise
A fistful too of sudden sorrows, a heaven filled with sighs

You're like a lesson that we learned with all our little friends,
And like these swallows as they leave, when summer ends

You're like a runway set for flight, they've cut your wings
    from you –
After you've fallen, and the vultures, your wings renew.

یک مشت کاغذ، پشت جلدت سرخ عنابی

با تو سفر کردن پر از ترس است و بی‌تابی

هر بار اسمی را لب مرزی صدا کردن

هر بار عشقی را لب مرزی، رها کردن

تو دست‌ها و چشم‌های مادرم هستی

تو رنگ بغض لحظه‌های آخرم هستی

وقت پریدن، بال‌های آهنی داری

وقت نشستن، ابر داری، یا که می‌باری

تو نه خراسانی، نه تهرانی، نه استانبول

یک سرزمین مبهمی، جا مانده پشت پل

تو هیچ جا و هر کجا که می‌روم هستی

در هوشیاری، خواب، در دیوانه‌گی، مستی

هی نخ به نخ، در ریه‌هایم زندگی کردی

حالا فقط یا سرفه‌ای، یا توده‌ی دردی

هر روز هر جا می‌روم زیر همین باران

ده بار می‌گویم: ولی . . . ای کاش . . . در ایران . . .

These bundled pages with their cover, purplish-red,*
Traveling with you is an impatience filled with dread

Calling your name at every border crossing,
Letting love go at every border crossing

You are my mother's hands, you are her eyes,
You are the color of my grief, my parting sighs

When I must fly, your wings are made of iron,
When I must land you're clouds, or you are rain

You're neither Khorasan, Tehran, or Istanbul –
Land left beyond a bridge now, vague and doubtful . . .

You're nowhere, and you're everywhere I go
You're waking, sleeping, in my madness, in my sorrow

You've made a life within my lungs, you're threaded there
And now you're just a cough, a lump of pain and care

And every day, and everywhere I go, beneath this rain,
Ten times I say, "But yet . . . I wish . . . and in Iran again . . ."

⌒

---

* The color of the Iranian passport.

ریشه‌ها

من باری درختی بودم
با کلاغ‌های سیاه و سفید در موهایم
با ریشه‌های وارونه‌ام
زمین بدنم را رها کرده بود
بدنم ریشه‌هایم را
ریشه‌هایی که پناه کلاغان بود
من باری همه بودم
رویایی پر جان در سال قحطی.

ROOTS

Once I was a tree
with black and white crows in my hair
with upside-down roots
the ground had set my body free,
my body, my roots,
roots that were the crows' refuge
once I was everything
a dream filled with life in a year of famine.

Lightning Source UK Ltd.
Milton Keynes UK
UKOW04f0809080116

265984UK00002B/12/P